How to use this journal

1. This journal is meant to kickstart your creative juices to create your own art that honors our Lord Jesus Christ.

2. There are 365 prompts designed for everyday of the year. Draw one prompt a day.

3. After drawing, take a moment to pray and meditate over what you drew - you will find that art is a wonderful tool that brings you closer to God.

4. The prompts for the first half of the journal are meant to be short detailed prompts while the latter half are bible verses that give you room for interpretation - so you may create more abstract artwork later. You'll get better at drawing halfway through, so the verses will give you more of a challenge!

5. Lastly feel free to take a picture and email your favorite artwork to EAowls@gmail.com--we will post them on 365christianprompts.com as well as possibly include it in a new illustrated bible where the funds are dedicated to charities and churches.

Blessings,

EA Owl

Old Testament

Ark of Covenant

High Priest

Tower of Babel

Destruction of Sodom

Burning Bush

Moses in the Basket

Crossing the Red-Sea

Bronze Serpent

Water from the Rock

Ten Commandments

Golden Calf

The Alter

Samson and the Lion

Shepherd Boy

David and Goliath

Murdered Abel

Noah's Ark

Great Flood

Rainbow of Covenant

Daniel in the Den

Daniel Praying

Three Hebrews

Unscarred by the Flame

King's Image

Sacrifice of Isaac

Father Abraham

Aaron the High-Priest

Adam and Eve

Forbidden Tree

Garden of Eden

King Solomon

Jacob Dreaming

Esau the Hunter

Rebecca at the Well

Joseph the Dreamer

Joseph in the Pit

Jacob and the Angel

Plague of Blood

Plague of Frogs

Plague of Boils

Plague of Locusts

Lord's Passover

Quail and Manna

Prophets of Baal

Chariot of Fire

Talking Donkey

Elisha

Sacrifice of Isaac

The Sons of Jacob

Pillar of Salt

Pharaoh's Dream

Joseph a Ruler

Rod of Moses

A leper

A Levite

Spies from Canaan

Trial of Job

Samson and Delilah

Death of Samson

Ruth in the Field

David Anointed

Queen of Sheba

Memorial Stones

New Testament

Jesus in the Manger

Walking on Water

Jesus Baptized

Sea of Galilee

Peter the Fisherman

Jesus Betrayed

Jesus in Trial

Jesus Crucified

Resurrected Christ

Last Supper

Empty Tomb

John the Baptist

Day of Pentecost

Blind Bartholomew

Zaccheaus on the Tree

Jesus Transfigured

Triumphal Entry

Jesus in the Temple

Jesus in Gethsemane

Jesus in the Wilderness

Jesus with the Disciples

Throne of God

Good Samaritan

Prodigal Son

Marriage of the Lamb

Ascending Christ

Resurrected Lazarus

The Day of Pentecost

Descending Dove

Martyred Stephen

Conversion of Saul

Peter in Prison

Peter with Cornelius

The Lamp-stand

Host of Angels

Twenty-four Elders

Book of Life

Lamb of God

The Gates of Heaven

Beast from the Sea

Four Horsemen

New Heaven

King Herod

Lake of Fire

Judgment Throne

Heavenly Worship

Disciples in the Tempest

Peter on Water

Preaching at Pentecost

Paul Shipwrecked

Paul and Silas

Jesus at the Well

Wedding at Cana

Cleansing the Temple

Christ Appears

Denial of Peter

The Rich Fool

Lord of Sabbath

Call of Simon

Anointing at Bethany

A Pharisee

John Beheaded

Ten Virgins

Jerusalem

Eating with sinners

Jesus tempted

River of Life

The Fig Tree

Lepers Cleansed

Narrow Way

False Prophets

Healing the Sick

Holy Communion

Praying Saints

Feeding the Poor

Travelling Pilgrim

The Street of Gold

Rapture

Aeneas Healed

Repent or Perish

Making Peace

A Boy Healed

A Tempted Man

Miracle

Poor Widow

Archangel

Antichrist

Lucifer

Cherubim

Forgiven

Love

Never Worry

Teamwork

Compromising

Apocalypse

Rewarded

The Lord's Day

Stewardship

Faithful

Humility

Repentance

Restitution

Persecuted

Famous Bible Verses

John 3:16 For God so loved the world that he gave his one and only Son, that whoever believes in him shall not perish but have eternal life.

John 1:1 In the beginning was the Word, and the Word was with God, and the Word was God.

John 14:6 Jesus answered, "I am the way and the truth and the life. No one comes to the Father except through me."

Matthew 28:19 Therefore go and make disciples of all nations, baptizing them in the name of the Father and of the Son and of the Holy Spirit.

Romans 3:23 For all have sinned and fall short of the glory of God.

Ephesians 2:8 For it is by grace you have been saved, through faith – and this is not from yourselves, it is the gift of God

Genesis 1:1 In the beginning God created the heavens and the earth.

Acts 1:8 "But you will receive power when the Holy Spirit comes on you; and you will be my witnesses in Jerusalem, and in all Judea and Samaria, and to the ends of the earth."

2 Timothy 3:16 All Scripture is God-breathed and is useful for teaching, rebuking, correcting and training in righteousness.

Romans 10:9 If you declare with your mouth, "Jesus is Lord," and believe in your heart that God raised him from the dead, you will be saved.

Romans 6:23 For the wages of sin is death, but the gift of God is eternal life in Christ Jesus our Lord.

Acts 2:38 Peter replied, "Repent and be baptized, every one of you, in the name of Jesus Christ for the forgiveness of your sins. And you will receive the gift of the Holy Spirit."

John 1:12 Yet to all who did receive him, to those who believed in his name, he gave the right to become children of God.

Romans 8:28 And we know that in all things God works for the good of those who love him, who have been called according to his purpose.

John 1:9 The true light that gives light to everyone was coming into the world.

Genesis 1:26 Then God said, "Let us make human beings in our image, in our likeness, so that they may rule over the fish in the sea and the birds in the sky, over the livestock and all the wild animals, and over all the creatures that move along the ground."

Romans 12:1 Therefore, I urge you, brothers and sisters, in view of God's mercy, to offer your bodies as a living sacrifice, holy and pleasing to God – this is true worship.

Romans 5:8 But God demonstrates his own love for us in this: While we were still sinners, Christ died for us.

Matthew 28:18 Then Jesus came to them and said, "All authority in heaven and on earth has been given to me."

John 3:3 Jesus replied, "Very truly I tell you, no one can see the kingdom of God without being born again."

Mark 16:15 He said to them, "Go into all the world and preach the gospel to all creation."

John 10:10 The thief comes only to steal and kill and destroy; I have come that they may have life, and have it to the full.

John 10:10 The thief comes only to steal and kill and destroy; I have come that they may have life, and have it to the full.

Acts 4:12 "Salvation is found in no one else, for there is no other name given under heaven by which we must be saved."

Acts 2:42 They devoted themselves to the apostles' teaching and to fellowship, to the breaking of bread and to prayer.

John 3:1 Now there was a Pharisee, a man named Nicodemus who was a member of the Jewish ruling council.

Galatians 5:22 But the fruit of the Spirit is love, joy, peace, patience, kindness, goodness, faithfulness

Proverbs 3:5 Trust in the LORD with all your heart and lean not on your own understanding.

Jeremiah 29:11 For I know the plans I have for you," declares the LORD, "plans to prosper you and not to harm you, plans to give you hope and a future.

John 2:1 On the third day a wedding took place at Cana in Galilee. Jesus' mother was there.

Titus 3:5 He saved us, not because of righteous things we had done, but because of his mercy. He saved us through the washing of rebirth and renewal by the Holy Spirit.

Romans 12:2 Do not conform to the pattern of this world, but be transformed by the renewing of your mind. Then you will be able to test and approve what God's will is – his good, pleasing and perfect will.

John 14:1 "Do not let your hearts be troubled. Trust in God; trust also in me."

John 4:1 Now Jesus learned that the Pharisees had heard that he was gaining and baptizing more disciples than John.

Ephesians 4:11 So Christ himself gave the apostles, the prophets, the evangelists, the pastors and teachers.

Romans 5:12 Therefore, just as sin entered the world through one man, and death through sin, and in this way death came to all people, because all sinned.

Matthew 11:28 "Come to me, all you who are weary and burdened, and I will give you rest."

Romans 5:1 Therefore, since we have been justified through faith, we have peace with God through our Lord Jesus Christ.

Genesis 1:27 So God created human beings in his own image, in the image of God he created them; male and female he created them.

Romans 1:16 I am not ashamed of the gospel, because it is the power of God that brings salvation to everyone who believes: first to the Jew, then to the Gentile.

1 John 1:9 If we confess our sins, he is faithful and just and will forgive us our sins and purify us from all unrighteousness.

Acts 2:1 When the day of Pentecost came, they were all together in one place.

2 Corinthians 5:17 Therefore, if anyone is in Christ, the new creation has come: The old has gone, the new is here!

Hebrews 11:1 Now faith is being sure of what we hope for and certain of what we do not see.

2 Timothy 2:15 Do your best to present yourself to God as one approved, a worker who does not need to be ashamed and who correctly handles the word of truth.

Romans 8:1 Therefore, there is now no condemnation for those who are in Christ Jesus.

Romans 10:13 For, "Everyone who calls on the name of the Lord will be saved."

John 8:32 "Then you will know the truth, and the truth will set you free."

Isaiah 9:6 For to us a child is born, to us a son is given, and the government will be on his shoulders. And he will be called Wonderful Counselor, Mighty God, Everlasting Father, Prince of Peace.

John 14:15 "If you love me, keep my commands."

Deuteronomy 6:4 Hear, O Israel: The LORD our God, the LORD is one.

John 13:34 "A new command I give you: Love one another. As I have loved you, so you must love one another."

John 4:24 "God is spirit, and his worshipers must worship in the Spirit and in truth."

Philippians 4:13 I can do all this through him who gives me strength.

Ephesians 2:1 As for you, you were dead in your transgressions and sins.

John 14:16 And I will ask the Father, and he will give you another advocate to help you and be with you forever.

Genesis 1:2 Now the earth was formless and empty, darkness was over the surface of the deep, and the Spirit of God was hovering over the waters.

Hebrews 4:12 For the word of God is alive and active. Sharper than any double-edged sword, it penetrates even to dividing soul and spirit, joints and marrow; it judges the thoughts and attitudes of the heart.

James 5:16 Therefore confess your sins to each other and pray for each other so that you may be healed. The prayer of a righteous person is powerful and effective.

Isaiah 7:14 Therefore the Lord himself will give you a sign: The virgin will conceive and give birth to a son, and will call him Immanuel.

John 1:7 He came as a witness to testify concerning that light, so that through him all might believe.

John 3:5 Jesus answered, "Very truly I tell you, no one can enter the kingdom of God without being born of water and the Spirit."

Philippians 2:5 In your relationships with one another, have the same attitude of mind Christ Jesus had.

John 1:29 The next day John saw Jesus coming toward him and said, "Look, the Lamb of God, who takes away the sin of the world!"

Romans 1:18 The wrath of God is being revealed from heaven against all the godlessness and wickedness of human beings who suppress the truth by their wickedness.

Philippians 4:6 Do not be anxious about anything, but in every situation, by prayer and petition, with thanksgiving, present your requests to God.

Hebrews 12:1 Therefore, since we are surrounded by such a great cloud of witnesses, let us throw off everything that hinders and the sin that so easily entangles. And let us run with perseverance the race marked out for us.

John 1:3 Through him all things were made; without him nothing was made that has been made.

Matthew 16:18 And I tell you that you are Peter, and on this rock I will build my church, and the gates of death will not overcome it.

Acts 17:11 Now the Berean Jews were of more noble character than those in Thessalonica, for they received the message with great eagerness and examined the Scriptures every day to see if what Paul said was true.

Galatians 2:20 I have been crucified with Christ and I no longer live, but Christ lives in me. The life I now live in the body, I live by faith in the Son of God, who loved me and gave himself for me.

Matthew 25:31 "When the Son of Man comes in his glory, and all the angels with him, he will sit on his glorious throne."

Matthew 5:17 "Do not think that I have come to abolish the Law or the Prophets; I have not come to abolish them but to fulfill them."

Romans 10:17 Consequently, faith comes from hearing the message, and the message is heard through the word about Christ.

Matthew 6:33 But seek first his kingdom and his righteousness, and all these things will be given to you as well.

Luke 4:18 "The Spirit of the Lord is on me, because he has anointed me to proclaim good news to the poor. He has sent me to proclaim freedom for the prisoners and recovery of sight for the blind, to set the oppressed free."

John 16:13 But when he, the Spirit of truth, comes, he will guide you into all the truth. He will not speak on his own; he will speak only what he hears, and he will tell you what is yet to come.

Acts 20:28 Keep watch over yourselves and all the flock of which the Holy Spirit has made you overseers. Be shepherds of the church of God, which he bought with his own blood.

Titus 2:11 For the grace of God has appeared that offers salvation to all people.

John 8:44 You belong to your father, the devil, and you want to carry out your father's desires. He was a murderer from the beginning, not holding to the truth, for there is no truth in him. When he lies, he speaks his native language, for he is a liar and the father of lies.

Ephesians 6:10 Finally, be strong in the Lord and in his mighty power.

Romans 13:1 Let everyone be subject to the governing authorities, for there is no authority except that which God has established. The authorities that exist have been established by God.

John 2:15 So he made a whip out of cords, and drove all from the temple courts, both sheep and cattle; he scattered the coins of the money changers and overturned their tables.

Mark 16:16 Whoever believes and is baptized will be saved, but whoever does not believe will be condemned.

Romans 3:10 As it is written: "There is no one righteous, not even one;"

Genesis 3:15 "And I will put enmity between you and the woman, and between your offspring and hers; he will crush your head, and you will strike his heel."

Hebrews 11:6 And without faith it is impossible to please God, because anyone who comes to him must believe that he exists and that he rewards those who earnestly seek him.

John 14:26 But the Advocate, the Holy Spirit, whom the Father will send in my name, will teach you all things and will remind you of everything I have said to you.

John 5:24 "Very truly I tell you, whoever hears my word and believes him who sent me has eternal life and will not be judged but has crossed over from death to life."

Joel 2:28 "And afterward, I will pour out my Spirit on all people. Your sons and daughters will prophesy, your old men will dream dreams, your young men will see visions."

Genesis 1:11 Then God said, "Let the land produce vegetation: seed-bearing plants and trees on the land that bear fruit with seed in it, according to their various kinds." And it was so.

James 1:2 Consider it pure joy, my brothers and sisters, whenever you face trials of many kinds.

Colossians 1:15 The Son is the image of the invisible God, the firstborn over all creation.

Titus 2:13 While we wait for the blessed hope – the appearing of the glory of our great God and Savior, Jesus Christ.

Philippians 4:8 Finally, brothers and sisters, whatever is true, whatever is noble, whatever is right, whatever is pure, whatever is lovely, whatever is admirable – if anything is excellent or praiseworthy – think about such things.

Acts 1:9 After he said this, he was taken up before their very eyes, and a cloud hid him from their sight.

John 4:7 When a Samaritan woman came to draw water, Jesus said to her, "Will you give me a drink?"

Micah 6:8 He has shown all you people what is good. And what does the LORD require of you? To act justly and to love mercy and to walk humbly with your God.

John 17:17 Sanctify them by the truth; your word is truth.

Leviticus 18:22 "Do not have sexual relations with a man as one does with a woman; that is detestable."

Acts 20:7 On the first day of the week we came together to break bread. Paul spoke to the people and, because he intended to leave the next day, kept on talking until midnight.

Acts 16:31 They replied, "Believe in the Lord Jesus, and you will be saved – you and your household."

John 11:25 Jesus said to her, "I am the resurrection and the life. Anyone who believes in me will live, even though they die."

John 8:58 "Very truly I tell you," Jesus answered, "before Abraham was born, I am!"

Acts 2:4 All of them were filled with the Holy Spirit and began to speak in other tongues as the Spirit enabled them.

John 15:5 "I am the vine; you are the branches. If you remain in me and I in you, you will bear much fruit; apart from me you can do nothing."

Acts 2:41 Those who accepted his message were baptized, and about three thousand were added to their number that day.

Proverbs 22:6 Start children off on the way they should go, and even when they are old they will not turn from it.

Genesis 3:1 Now the serpent was more crafty than any of the wild animals the LORD God had made. He said to the woman, "Did God really say, 'You must not eat from any tree in the garden'?"

James 1:5 If any of you lacks wisdom, you should ask God, who gives generously to all without finding fault, and it will be given to you.

Hebrews 1:1 In the past God spoke to our ancestors through the prophets at many times and in various ways

2 John 1:2 Because of the truth, which lives in us and will be with us forever.

John 17:3 Now this is eternal life: that they know you, the only true God, and Jesus Christ, whom you have sent.

Luke 16:19 "There was a rich man who was dressed in purple and fine linen and lived in luxury every day."

John 5:7 "Sir," the invalid replied, "I have no one to help me into the pool when the water is stirred. While I am trying to get in, someone else goes down ahead of me."

John 8:31 To the Jews who had believed him, Jesus said, "If you hold to my teaching, you are really my disciples."

Luke 1:4 So that you may know the certainty of the things you have been taught.

Revelation 3:20 Here I am! I stand at the door and knock. If anyone hears my voice and opens the door, I will come in and eat with them, and they with me.

1 Peter 2:3 Now that you have tasted that the Lord is good.

John 10:30 "I and the Father are one."

1 Peter 3:15 But in your hearts revere Christ as Lord. Always be prepared to give an answer to everyone who asks you to give the reason for the hope that you have. But do this with gentleness and respect.

Matthew 7:21 "Not everyone who says to me, 'Lord, Lord,' will enter the kingdom of heaven, but only those who do the will of my Father who is in heaven."

John 3:18 Whoever believes in him is not condemned, but whoever does not believe stands condemned already because they have not believed in the name of God's one and only Son.

Genesis 12:1 The LORD had said to Abram, "Go from your country, your people and your father's household to the land I will show you."

John 3:8 "The wind blows wherever it pleases. You hear its sound, but you cannot tell where it comes from or where it is going. So it is with everyone born of the Spirit."

John 15:1 "I am the true vine, and my Father is the gardener."

Genesis 2:7 Then the LORD God formed a man from the dust of the ground and breathed into his nostrils the breath of life, and the man became a living being.

Genesis 1:3 And God said, "Let there be light," and there was light.

John 8:12 When Jesus spoke again to the people, he said, "I am the light of the world. Whoever follows me will never walk in darkness, but will have the light of life."

1 Peter 2:9 But you are a chosen people, a royal priesthood, a holy nation, God's special possession, that you may declare the praises of him who called you out of darkness into his wonderful light.

Luke 1:26 In the sixth month of Elizabeth's pregnancy, God sent the angel Gabriel to Nazareth, a town in Galilee.

Hebrews 9:27 Just as people are destined to die once, and after that to face judgment.

John 3:2 He came to Jesus at night and said, "Rabbi, we know that you are a teacher who has come from God. For no one could perform the signs you are doing if God were not with him."

Matthew 5:14 "You are the light of the world. A city on a hill cannot be hidden."

1 Corinthians 6:9 Or do you not know that wrongdoers will not inherit the kingdom of God? Do not be deceived:

Neither the sexually immoral nor idolaters nor adulterers nor male prostitutes nor practicing homosexuals.

Luke 10:25 On one occasion an expert in the law stood up to test Jesus. "Teacher," he asked, "what must I do to inherit eternal life?"

Matthew 7:7 "Ask and it will be given to you; seek and you will find; knock and the door will be opened to you."

John 1:8 He himself was not the light; he came only as a witness to the light.

Ephesians 1:3 Praise be to the God and Father of our Lord Jesus Christ, who has blessed us in the heavenly realms with every spiritual blessing in Christ.

Matthew 1:18 This is how the birth of Jesus the Messiah came about: His mother Mary was pledged to be married to Joseph, but before they came together, she was found to be pregnant through the Holy Spirit.

Romans 1:20 For since the creation of the world God's invisible qualities – his eternal power and divine nature – have been clearly seen, being understood from what has been made, so that people are without excuse.

John 8:9 At this, those who heard began to go away one at a time, the older ones first, until only Jesus was left, with the woman still standing there.

John 1:5 The light shines in the darkness, and the darkness has not overcome it.

1 Thessalonians 4:13 Brothers and sisters, we do not want you to be uninformed about those who sleep in death, so that you do not grieve like the rest, who have no hope.

Hebrews 13:5 Keep your lives free from the love of money and be content with what you have, because God has said,

"Never will I leave you; never will I forsake you."

1 John 4:1 Dear friends, do not believe every spirit, but test the spirits to see whether they are from God, because many false prophets have gone out into the world. NIV

Matthew 22:37 Jesus replied: "Love the Lord your God with all your heart and with all your soul and with all your mind."

James 1:17 Every good and perfect gift is from above, coming down from the Father of the heavenly lights, who does not change like shifting shadows.

Matthew 6:19 "Do not store up for yourselves treasures on earth, where moth and rust destroy, and where thieves break in and steal."

Isaiah 61:1 The Spirit of the Sovereign LORD is on me, because the LORD has anointed me to proclaim good news to the poor. He has sent me to bind up the brokenhearted, to proclaim freedom for the captives and release from darkness for the prisoners.

Galatians 3:28 There is neither Jew nor Gentile, neither slave nor free, neither male nor female, for you are all one in Christ Jesus.

2 Peter 3:9 The Lord is not slow in keeping his promise, as some understand slowness. Instead he is patient with you, not wanting anyone to perish, but everyone to come to repentance.

Acts 1:11 "Men of Galilee," they said, "why do you stand here looking into the sky? This same Jesus, who has been taken from you into heaven, will come back in the same way you have seen him go into heaven."

James 5:14 Is anyone among you sick? Let them call the elders of the church to pray over them and anoint them with oil in the name of the Lord.

John 3:36 Whoever believes in the Son has eternal life, but whoever rejects the Son will not see life, for God's wrath remains on them.

Ephesians 6:12 For our struggle is not against flesh and blood, but against the rulers, against the authorities, against the powers of this dark world and against the spiritual forces of evil in the heavenly realms.

Matthew 6:9 "This, then, is how you should pray: "Our Father in heaven, hallowed be your name,"

Acts 3:19 Repent, then, and turn to God, so that your sins may be wiped out, that times of refreshing may come from the Lord.

James 2:14 What good is it, my brothers and sisters, if people claim to have faith but have no deeds? Can such faith save them?

Isaiah 40:31 But those who hope in the LORD will renew their strength. They will soar on wings like eagles; they will run and not grow weary, they will walk and not be faint.

John 3:17 For God did not send his Son into the world to condemn the world, but to save the world through him.

Luke 1:35 The angel answered, "The Holy Spirit will come on you, and the power of the Most High will overshadow you. So the holy one to be born will be called the Son of God."

Genesis 1:28 God blessed them and said to them, "Be fruitful and increase in number; fill the earth and subdue it. Rule over the fish in the sea and the birds in the sky and over every living creature that moves on the ground."

Ephesians 2:10 For we are God's handiwork, created in Christ Jesus to do good works, which God prepared in advance for us to do.

2 Corinthians 5:21 God made him who had no sin to be sin for us, so that in him we might become the righteousness of God.

Romans 6:1 What shall we say, then? Shall we go on sinning so that grace may increase?

Ephesians 1:13 And you also were included in Christ when you heard the word of truth, the gospel of your salvation. When you believed, you were marked in him with a seal, the promised Holy Spirit

Romans 6:3 Or don't you know that all of us who were baptized into Christ Jesus were baptized into his death?

Matthew 18:15 "If a brother or sister sins, go and point out the fault, just between the two of you. If they listen to you, you have won them over."

1 John 4:5 They are from the world and therefore speak from the viewpoint of the world, and the world listens to them.

Luke 2:1 In those days Caesar Augustus issued a decree that a census should be taken of the entire Roman world.

James 1:27 Religion that God our Father accepts as pure and faultless is this: to look after orphans and widows in their distress and to keep oneself from being polluted by the world.

John 16:33 "I have told you these things, so that in me you may have peace. In this world you will have trouble. But take heart! I have overcome the world."

John 5:28 "Do not be amazed at this, for a time is coming when all who are in their graves will hear his voice"

John 5:39 You study the Scriptures diligently because you think that in them you possess eternal life. These are the very Scriptures that testify about me.

Titus 2:3 Likewise, teach the older women to be reverent in the way they live, not to be slanderers or addicted to much wine, but to teach what is good.

John 4:23 Yet a time is coming and has now come when the true worshipers will worship the Father in the Spirit and in truth, for they are the kind of worshipers the Father seeks.

Matthew 7:1 "Do not judge, or you too will be judged."

1 Timothy 2:5 For there is one God and one mediator between God and human beings, Christ Jesus, himself human.

Matthew 4:1 Then Jesus was led by the Spirit into the wilderness to be tempted by the devil.

John 1:18 No one has ever seen God, but the one and only Son, who is himself God and is in closest relationship with the Father, has made him known.

John 5:1 Some time later, Jesus went up to Jerusalem for one of the Jewish festivals.

Ephesians 5:18 Do not get drunk on wine, which leads to debauchery. Instead, be filled with the Spirit.

Ephesians 5:22 Wives, submit yourselves to your own husbands as you do to the Lord.

Revelation 21:1 Then I saw "a new heaven and a new earth," for the first heaven and the first earth had passed away, and there was no longer any sea.

Micah 5:2 "But you, Bethlehem Ephrathah, though you are small among the clans of Judah, out of you will come for me one who will be ruler over Israel, whose origins are from of old, from ancient times."

2 Peter 3:4 They will say, "Where is this 'coming' he promised? Ever since our ancestors died, everything goes on as it has since the beginning of creation."

John 6:44 "No one can come to me unless the Father who sent me draws them, and I will raise them up at the last day."

Genesis 2:18 The LORD God said, "It is not good for the man to be alone. I will make a helper suitable for him."

Psalms 119:105 Your word is a lamp to my feet and a light for my path.

Made in the USA
Coppell, TX
03 July 2022